Take opportunities
to chase your
own adventures!

Mandy M. Kim

Ava

A Year of Adventure in the Life of an American Avocet

Meadowlark Press, llc
Emporia, Kansas USA

American Avocet

\ ˈavəˌset \

Recurvirostra americana

(recurvi = "curving upward" and rostra = "bird's bill," from America)

Length: 16.9-18.5 inches

Weight: 9.7-12.3 ounces

Wingspan: 28.4 inches

Published by
Meadowlark Press, LLC
PO BOX 333, Emporia, Kansas, USA
www.meadowlark-books.com

ISBN 978-1-7362232-3-9 (hardcover)
ISBN 978-1-7362232-4-6 (paperback)

Library of Congress Control Number
2021935418

The Kansas Wetlands Education Center is dedicated to educating the public about wetland communities, their importance, and the need for conservation and restoration, with emphasis on Cheyenne Bottoms and Quivira National Wildlife Refuge. KWEC accomplishes this through interactive exhibits and interpretation, education programs, outreach, and fostering partnerships with cooperating stakeholders. The KWEC, 592 NE K-156 Highway, is at the southeast side of Cheyenne Bottoms Wildlife Area, northeast of Great Bend, Kansas. Visit https://wetlandscenter.fhsu.edu for more information.

Ava: A Year of Adventure in the Life of an American Avocet was made possible by funds from the Dorothy M. Morrison Foundation, a private foundation serving the Barton County, Kansas area.

Photos in this book provided by Wendell Hinkson, Kansas Department of Wildlife, Parks & Tourism, Jonas Kern, Joseph Kern, Mandy Kern, Park Elementary Drone Club, Joseph Thomasson, and Dan Witt. Laura Chamberlin created the WHSRN map.

Supplemental materials for the classroom available at https://wetlandscenter.fhsu.edu/education
Lexile Range: 1010L-1200L

CATALOGING DATA:

Ava: A Year of Adventure in the Life of an American Avocet / [story by] Mandy Kern / [illustrations by] Onalee Nicklin /

JNF051100   **JUVENILE NONFICTION** / Science & Nature / Environmental Science & Ecosystems

NAT043000   **NATURE** / Animals / Birds

SCI070060   **SCIENCE** / Life Sciences / Zoology / Ethology (Animal Behavior)

As the sun rose over the Laguna Madre, which stretches along the coast of Texas and Mexico, the elegant Ava preened, anxiously awaiting her adventure.

Ava is an American Avocet.

She shares her winter home with hundreds of thousands of shorebirds in one of six LAGOONS in the world that is saltier than the ocean.

The birds navigate the MANGROVES in the HYPERSALINE water, gathering and readying for spring MIGRATION.

Ava looked around the ESTUARY, rich with FLORA and FAUNA. Crabs, shrimp, and fish were plentiful in the shallow stands of seagrass.

Even though she could see everything that the wetland provided, Ava felt a pull to fly north with the other Avocets to find mates, food, and nesting ground. MIGRATION can be difficult. Storms, loss of HABITAT, and even power lines can be hazards — but it was time to leave her beloved Laguna Madre in the Gulf of Mexico.

Avocets are not marathon fliers and migrate only medium-range distances at a time. The ALGAL MATS at the Salt Plains National Wildlife Refuge in Oklahoma provide an opportunity to rest and feed for not only the Avocets, now 800 miles from their winter grounds, but also for Willets, Greater Yellowlegs, and Sanderlings. All could be seen foraging for INVERTEBRATES in the BIOFILM of the shallow pools.

Ava's adventures continued for another 200 miles.

Ava was ready to stop for a rest on a dreary morning flight when the clouds in front of her cleared. She saw an amazing site. A huge wetland ECOSYSTEM was calling her down. This was the 41,000-acre, freshwater MARSH called Cheyenne Bottoms in the middle of Kansas. As she slowed and circled, she took note of her surroundings. In a sea of CATTAILS, Great Blue Herons, Double-crested Cormorants, and Great Egrets greeted her as she landed.

Waterfowl Flyways

Atlantic
Mississippi
Central
Pacific

Migratory birds like ducks, geese, and shorebirds follow instinctual pathways year after year from their breeding grounds to wintering areas.

As the largest wetland complex in the interior of the United States, Cheyenne Bottoms is a crucial stopping point on the Central Flyway for millions of birds during their annual migrations in the spring and fall. The surrounding 100-foot-high bluffs create a natural land-sink that captures water from area creeks. Its shallow pools and MUDFLATS make Cheyenne Bottoms the perfect habitat for shorebirds like Ava.

Functions of a Wetland

Critical wildlife habitat

Mixes oxygen and cycles nutrients

Reduces effects of erosion

Slows down flooding

Converts toxins

Captures sediment and filters toxins

Captures carbon

Soaks up excess water and releases slowly

Some Facts about Wetlands:

- In only 23 years, between 1955 and 1978, 40% of the wetlands in Kansas disappeared.

- Wetlands around the world are vanishing at a rate three times that of forests.

- Wetlands are one of the most biodiverse ecosystems on the planet, as varied and productive as rain forests and coral reefs.

- Wetlands do amazing things for their surrounding communities, such as reduce soil erosion by capturing sediment and soaking up extra flood water.

- The relatively calm wetland waters allow toxins to settle to the bottom, in effect, cleaning the water that flows out again. Wetland plants help by acting as traps or filters.

support more wildlife diversity than the remaining 99%.

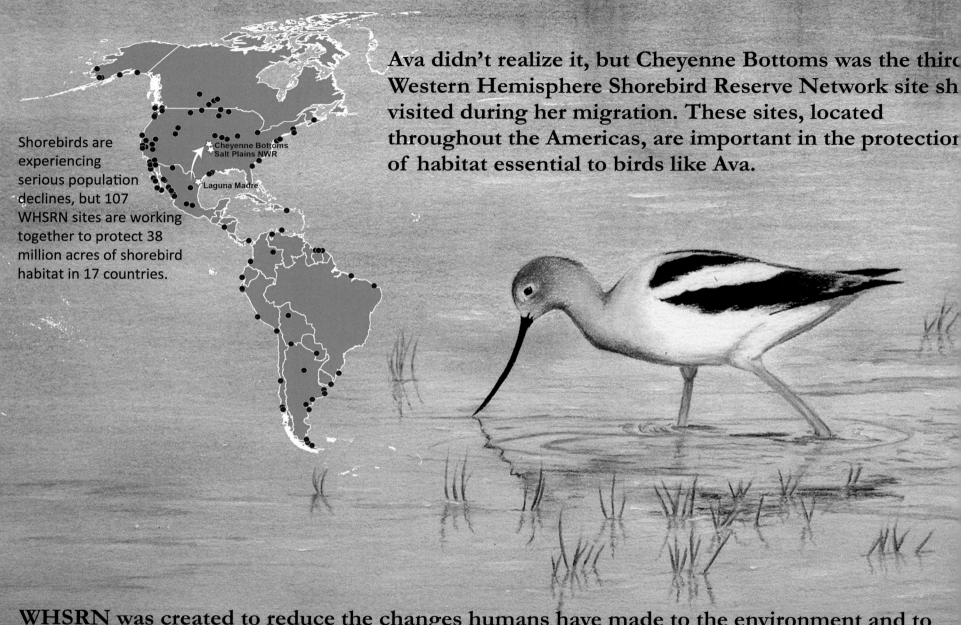

Ava didn't realize it, but Cheyenne Bottoms was the third Western Hemisphere Shorebird Reserve Network site sh[e] visited during her migration. These sites, located throughout the Americas, are important in the protection of habitat essential to birds like Ava.

Shorebirds are experiencing serious population declines, but 107 WHSRN sites are working together to protect 38 million acres of shorebird habitat in 17 countries.

Cheyenne Bottoms
Salt Plains NWR

Laguna Madre

WHSRN was created to reduce the changes humans have made to the environment and to ensure there are locations for birds to stop, rest, feed, and breed along their migration routes. Thankfully, the American Avocet is a species of low-conservation concern because their numbers are strong.

Ava surveyed her surroundings. There were so many different kinds of birds. The Long-billed Curlew was probing for worms with its impossibly long, thin, curved beak.

The Wilson's Phalaropes spun in circles, creating a vortex that brought their favorite snacks, aquatic invertebrates, to the surface.

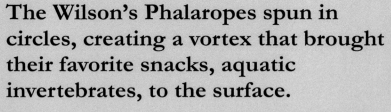

The sharp cries of "Killdeer, Killdeer" caught her attention as a tan bird with a white chest topped with two black bands shouted at a Speckled Kingsnake approaching its nest. The Killdeer's mate flopped away as if he had a broken wing, a trick to lure the snake away.

Ava knew the relief of the Hudsonian Godwit as it found a good feeding spot in the shallow water. Godwits fly thousands of miles nonstop, going days without rest, and they depend on Cheyenne Bottoms for a break and a meal before they continue on their journey further north.

What Ava did not notice was a spooked American Bittern who was CAMOUFLAGED amongst the BULRUSHES swaying in the breeze.

She watched as a flock of American White Pelicans herded fish and scooped them up, tilting their bills to swallow them whole.

This Wetland of International Importance is a welcome respite for so many migrant species.

Then, out of the corner of her eye, she noticed him with his rusty-colored head, his black and white wings, and bluish-gray legs. Ava stopped in her tracks, lowered her head, and extended her neck. She wanted to get to know him. This male Avocet started preening his wings and splashing water in a frenzy. He was signaling to Ava that they would be a perfect match. Circling, they started dancing, beak to beak, and he placed a wing on Ava's back.

Ava and her new mate waded to one of the raised islands in the marsh. They selected an area with very little vegetation, the male making several scrapes in the ground with his breast and feet until they both agreed on the perfect spot. They made more shallow depressions in the soil, and together they collected a few stems of smartweed. They found some beautiful white feathers a Snowy Egret left behind and finished decorating their humble nest with a few pebbles.

Over the next few days Ava laid four greenish-brown eggs with irregular dark brown and black spots. Each egg had one very pointed end, which is a trait of shorebird eggs. As they are laid on the ground in shallow nests, the shape prevents them from rolling out of the nest and off the island if they are bumped.

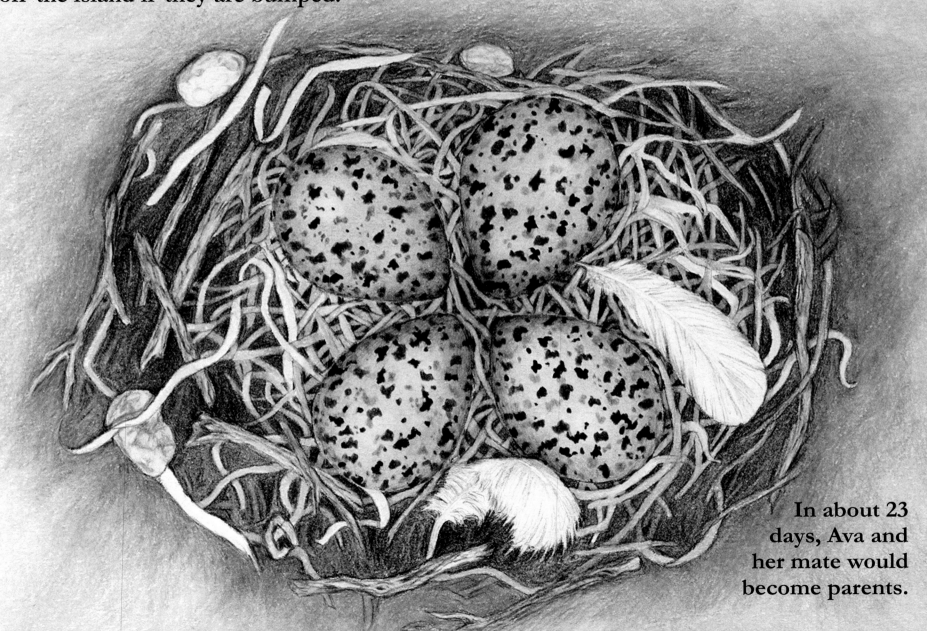

In about 23 days, Ava and her mate would become parents.

Male and female Avocets take turns INCUBATING and sitting on the nest during the day. As there were no trees or bushes to provide shade, she dipped her belly feathers in the water to help keep the eggs cool when the temperatures rose. Ava sat on the nest at night.

The next morning, they awoke to a howling wind. Rain came pelting down, down, and down some more. The water level began rising. Ava was scared. The island was disappearing. Ava and her mate rushed to gather sticks and find more feathers, working together frantically to raise the nest just enough to get the eggs to safety.

The rain continued all day, but the nest was safe. Their hustle had worked, and all was clear for the night.

Or was it?

Wetlands are important places for many animals, as well as bird[s]
Cheyenne Bottoms is home to at least 44 MAMMAL species.

Avocet eggs were on the midnight snack menu for this
raccoon. Ava was again in a fight to save her new family.

Crouching down and stretching out her neck, Ava extended her wings to their full two feet, ruffled her feathers, and ran directly at the raccoon. Her teetering gait surprised the critter, but even more startling was her shrill "KLEET KLEET KLEET" cry of alarm. It increased in pitch as she moved, making it sound as if she was approaching fast, quite the trick for an angry mama defending her nest.

It worked!

After three weeks of protection, care, and excitement, the day arrived. Four little DOWNY chicks peered over the edge of the nest. Within hours, the PRECOCIAL BROOD began testing out their long, awkward legs.

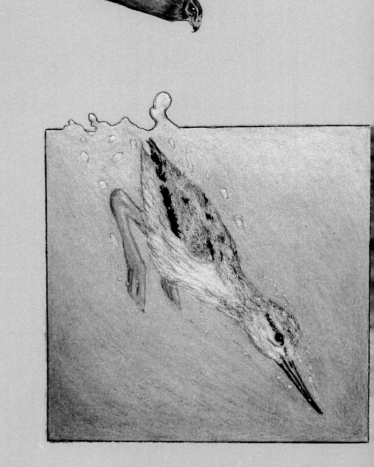

Out for a swim, the parents watched as the cinnamon-headed Avocet chicks dove under water when a Northern Harrier swooped down low, gliding over the wetlands, looking for prey. In a month, the chicks would be strong enough to fly off on their own adventures. Until then, both parents would watch over the young and teach them all they knew.

With the chicks able to feed themselves, the family set out in the muck of the flats in search of food. They mixed with a flock of Avocets near some Ring-billed Gulls.

The Avocets' slightly webbed, splayed feet moved through the water without disturbing it as the birds swept their heads from side to side, moving their beaks through the shallow water. They found their food by touch and pulled a mix of aquatic insects and crustaceans from the mud. A few Avocets could be seen plunging their heads under water, looking for prey. One even snatched a passing dragonfly right out of the sky.

Colonies of Black-necked Stilts also feed in the mud flats. This cousin to the American Avocet is very dignified in appearance with their tuxedo-like plumage and rosy pink legs. Stilt legs are the longest, relative to body size, of any North American bird.

Cheyenne Bottoms is abundant with food for its diverse population of guests.

Dragonfly NAIADS swim near the vegetation. Mayfly NYMPHS, in their last INSTAR stage, are MOLTING at the water's edge. Crayfish chimneys dot the banks.

Water Boatmen row their arms down the water column with a bubble of trapped air, allowing them to stay underwater for long periods of time. One little chick successfully tugs the LARVA of a non-biting Midge Fly out of the mud. These bloodworms are so dense that in the hot summer months, over 65,000 of the bright red macroinvertebrates can be found in each square meter of muck at Cheyenne Bottoms. That's 61 tons, or the equivalent of three dump trucks worth of food available each month.

No wonder shorebirds love Cheyenne Bottoms.

As summer neared an end, the chicks FLEDGED off on their own to join other juvenile Avocets. Ava noticed that her mate's rusty-colored head and neck, like her own, had molted to a striking grayish white.

Ava's adventures at Cheyenne Bottoms had come to an end. Even though she enjoyed the ample food supply and diversity of life the marsh provided, the harsh Kansas winter would be too much for an Avocet. It was time to migrate south for the winter.

Fall is an ever-changing scene at Cheyenne Bottoms. The rolling, trumpeting calls of the Sandhill Cranes as they pass overhead can be heard from miles away. The Greater White-fronted Geese arrive in droves, and Bald Eagles soon appear, following the incoming flocks of waterfowl. American Coots dot the landscape of the marsh, and the reptiles and amphibians of the wetland find safe places for their winter BRUMATION.

After a long flight south, Ava arrived at the Laguna Madre, pleased with her year of adventures.
Next spring, the cycle would begin again. Hundreds of American Avocets would embark to
Cheyenne Bottoms, some for a brief stay, migrating as far north as Canada, while others would
nest and start their own families among the reeds of this globally important bird area.

WHSRN Sites Ava Visited

Laguna Madre

Stretching almost 400 miles from Port Mansfield, Texas, to the Soto la Marina River in Tamaulipas, Mexico, the Laguna Madre was designated as an internationally important WHSRN site in 2000. Areas are managed by the US Fish and Wildlife Service, US National Park Service, Martinez Family, and the National Commission of Protected Natural Areas in Mexico. 1.6 million acres of habitat support more than 100,000 shorebirds. It is made up of a network of native grasslands, marshes, shallow bays, wind tidal flats, and barrier islands.

Salt Plains NWR

The Salt Plains National Wildlife Refuge in Oklahoma spans over 32,000 acres and became an internationally important WHSRN site in 1994. Partners include Cherokee Mainstreet, Friends of the Salt Plains NWR, Great Salt Plains State Park, and Oklahoma Department of Wildlife Conservation, and it is owned by the US Fish and Wildlife Service. Approximately 20% of the North American breeding population of Snowy Plovers depends on these salt flats, shorelines, and wetlands. There is a designated area on the salt flats where visitors can dig for selenite crystals, the only place in the world where they are found with hour-glass inclusions.

Cheyenne Bottoms

This 41,000-acre land sink, located in central Kansas, is considered the largest wetland complex in the interior of the United States. It was designated as a hemispherically important site in 1988 due to International Shorebird Surveys showing more than 500,000 shorebirds use the site. The Bottoms consists of a wildlife area owned by the State of Kansas and managed by the Kansas Department of Wildlife, Parks, and Tourism, and the Cheyenne Bottoms Preserve, owned and managed by The Nature Conservancy. The habitat is a mix of freshwater marsh and upland grass areas.

WHSRN
WESTERN HEMISPHERE
SHOREBIRD RESERVE NETWORK
/ wiz-ern /

Glossary

Algal /ˈalg(ə)l/ **Mats** – Bacteria colony that forms on the surface of water or rocks.

Biofilm – Tiny organisms that stick to each other and to surfaces like rocks and water. It is an important part of the food chain, providing nutrients for aquatic invertebrates on which shorebirds feed.

Brood – Family of chicks that hatches at the same time.

Brumation \ brü-ˈmā-shən \ – A period of dormancy reptiles and amphibians enter to conserve energy. Similar to hibernation in mammals.

Bulrush – Grassy wetland plant that grows in tall bunches along the waterline.

Camouflage \ ˈka-mə-ˌfläj \ – Patterns, coloring, and sometimes behavior that can help animals blend in with their surroundings. When spooked, the American Bittern will hold its bill straight up in the air and sway back and forth, blending in with the cattails.

Cattail – Marsh plant that is both wanted and unwanted. Many animals will use cattails to build their homes, but they can also spread rapidly and choke out other plants in the wetland.

Downy – Soft and fluffy first feathers of birds.

Ecosystem – Connected living organisms with the nonliving environment.

Estuary \ ˈes-chə-ˌwer-ē \ – An area where rivers or streams divide and spread as they connect to the ocean, depositing sediments collected along their route.

Fauna \ ˈfä-nə \ – The animals that live in a certain area make up its fauna. Cheyenne Bottoms is home to many species of birds, insects, mammals, amphibians, reptiles, and more.

Flora – The plant life that grows in a certain area make up its flora. Plants that grow in Cheyenne Bottoms must be adapted to growing in very wet conditions.

Fledge – When a young bird is covered in feathers necessary to fly and is ready to leave the nest. These birds are called fledglings.

Habitat – An area that contains all of the things necessary to support life for a particular animal.

Hypersaline – Very salty water. The Laguna Madre has a salt level of 36 parts per thousand. The average ocean water is 35 parts per thousand.

Incubating – Maintaining a specific temperature for the proper amount of time for an egg to hatch.

Instar – A stage of metamorphosis development in insects. Insects may go from egg to larva, to pupa, to adult, or may skip the pupal stage. Instar is the period of shedding the exoskeleton to the larger stage.

Invertebrates – Animals without a backbone. These include snails, insects, crayfish, clams, and many others.

Lagoon – Shallow body of water separated from a larger body of water by small patches of land.

Larva – The metamorphic stage of an insect after it hatches from an egg. It is typically wingless and wormlike.

Mammal – Warm blooded, vertebrate animal covered in fur or hair. Live young are fed the mother's milk.

Mangrove – Woody shrub found in coastal wetlands in tropical regions. These plants are specially adapted to growing in salty water.

Marsh — A type of wetland characterized by soft-stemmed plants.

Migration — During different seasons many animals, including birds, move from one location to another.

Molting — Birds lose old feathers to make way for new feathers. The American Avocet pair molted their breeding plumage (feathers) before heading back to Mexico.

Mudflats — Exposed areas of mud with little vegetation. Rain will create shallow pools.

Naiads \ ˈnā-əds \ and **Nymphs** \ ˈnim(p)fs \ Aquatic insect larva, such as those of dragonflies and mayflies, in early stages of their metamorphosis.

Precocial \ pri-ˈkō-shəl \ — Independent from birth. Once hatched, the American Avocet chicks are fully capable of movement and are able to feed themselves.

Preen — Birds use their beaks and bills to adjust feathers, apply oils produced near their tail to strengthen or waterproof feathers, and remove parasites.

The Laguna Madre is a narrow strip of water that separates the mainland of Texas and Mexico from a 400-mile-long island. This lagoon ecosystem is made up of a network of native grasslands, marshes, shallow bays, wind tidal flats, and barrier islands.

Oklahoma's Salt Plains National Wildlife Refuge spans more than 32,000 acres. The salt flats were made when a prehistoric ocean receded, trapping its salt water in this natural basin where the salt solidified as the water evaporated.

Plants of Cheyenne Bottoms

Wetland plants are specially adapted for growing in water in order to survive frequent floods. Cattails have aerenchyma cells—air tubes in their stems—that let air flow inside the plant, from the leaves to the roots.

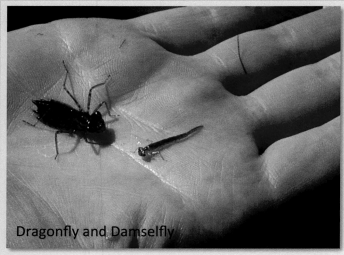

Dragonfly and Damselfly

Aquatic Invert Bioindicators

Biologists look for several species of aquatic invertebrates to tell whether a body of water is healthy or polluted. Young dragonflies, damselflies, stoneflies, mayflies, and dobsonflies are sensitive to pollutants, so their presence is a good sign.

Mayfly

Dobsonfly

The author expresses her appreciation to the KWEC staff—Curtis, Linda, Pam, Tom, and Jim—for their support. A special thanks to Rob Penner with The Nature Conservancy for helping with scientific accuracy and making connections with organizations committed to shorebird conservation. Author Mandy Kern is the Program Specialist at the Kansas Wetlands Education Center and dedicates this book to Joseph, Jonas, Russell, and Maggie, and thanks them for their encouragement, assistance, and love for all things outdoors.

Artist Onalee Nicklin thanks Mandy Kern and Tracy Million Simmons for inviting her to this project, her family for their ongoing support, and her husband, Timothy, for always encouraging her to do her best and pursue her dreams. She dedicates this artwork in memory of her Grandmother Clock, for passing on her artistic talent, love of nature, and especially, her love of birds.

Ramsar

The Ramsar Convention on Wetlands is an international treaty that guides countries on their conservation and wise use of wetlands. Birds don't know when they have crossed a border, so they rely on the cooperation of many countries to ensure that they have safe places to live. Cheyenne Bottoms was recognized by the Ramsar Convention in 1988 because a significant number of migratory shorebirds in North America spend time there each year.